HE TOOK THE PAIN B

# HE TOOK THE PAIN BUT LEFT THE

# MEMORIES

GREGORY D. PATTERSON

Copyright © 2015. Gregory D. Patterson. All rights reserved.

ISBN: 150848273X

ISBN-13: 978-1508482734


Published by:

Ellis & Ellis Consulting Group, LLC

www.ellisandellisconsulting.org

info@ellisandellisconsulting.org

(678)-438-3574 / 242-347-2347

# <u>DEDICATION</u>

To my nephew Jordan Clark

My entire family, Bishop Hezekiah Walker and Love Fellowship Tabernacle, Southern Grove Baptist Church, Dr. A.H. Jones, Dr. Charles Gray and Mount Olive Baptist Church, St. Luke Baptist Church, Bishop Herman Murray and Full Gospel Holy Temple, Scotland County and surrounding area churches, German Bostic, Terrance Bradham, Corey Chambers, Raymond Warren, Towanda Crawford, Jackie Phillips, Matthew Dunigan, Adrian Blackmon, Pastor Kirvy Brown and my godson's Luwan and CJ.

In Loving Memory of: James Patterson (dad), Willie P. Mclean Sr., Hazel Patterson, Maggie Patterson, Sallie Stubbs, Lonnie Stubbs Sr.

# ENDORSEMENTS

Praying that God fills you back up to pour back into the people man, I support and endorse your ministry! #certified

*Dr. Earnest Pugh*

From trials to tribulation and back. Gregory Patterson not only fought to survive but he stood on every word God promised him. This book will touch many lives because he comes from a place where many have not gone and where others are trying to get to. He is a great man of God with a great destiny and this is his birthing season. And I'm honored to know him.

*Jamila A. White*

Whether a believer or not this book will question fundamental truths of whether God is real because every fiber in you will come to the conclusion that something supernatural was at work. I choose to believe that it will be apparent after reading these true events for even the non-believers there will stir a hint of truth that God reigns and it's with great pleasure that I endorse not only an awesome read which has the core elements of emotions, but penetrates the very values of the heart hidden from view.

*Terry E. Lyle, Author*

# CONTENTS

# INTRODUCTION

The discovery of one's peculiarity is one like no other. Such a discovery can be likened to figuring out a mystery you didn't know existed. Finding out that you are peculiar is the moment that you realize that although you are in so many ways just like the next person, you are still set apart from the rest. There is an innate voice embedded in the deep places of your core that whispers a resounding message that says "you are different." Before you know, you believe these words and pursue the truth that comes with them.

At a significantly early age--14 years young to be exact--it had become very clear to me that I was cut from a rare fabric. It wasn't by choice, it was by calling. The truth is that I didn't choose to be different, I was called to be different. I was chosen to sing, preach, teach, and perpetuate the good news of Jesus Christ to the world. For me, it was by destiny and not by default. Perhaps that is why giving God a sure "yes" came so natural for me. I was intrigued that a God who owned the world would trust me to bring His name glory in it.

In a world where everyone conforms to the norms of society and culture, you can imagine the price of walking into this call came with. *Misunderstood. Rejected. Scrutinized.* Deciding to not be the "average" guy my age wasn't easily accepted by those around me. Some thought instead of exploring a life with God, I should have given my focus to being young, wild, and free. It would have made some people love me more if I choice the club over the church. Even if I desired to do so, I couldn't shake the divine pull that was leading me to a life submitted in God.

To be welcomed by my peers or those that I would have appreciated acceptance from would have been good to have, I won't deny that. Because after all, who can say that they don't expect approval from the outside and it actually be true? Not many; and assuredly not me.

When I realized what being me would entail, it became necessary for me to take a firm grip to what God thought of me and what He had planned for me. God's idea of me became the identity that I owned. In my heart, mind, and soul, I had to let that be enough. If not, I would lose myself and the call on my life at the expense of trying to be found in good standing with everyone in my environment.

I want to tell you that being called made me immune to humanness, but it didn't. If I told you that living life peculiarly made pain inescapable, I would be telling a lie that's as far from the truth as the oceans are from the sky. The truth of it all is, my calling didn't come without crucifixion. The same God that trusted me to serve also allowed me to suffer, but what I adore the most is, the same way in which suffering was not withheld from me, neither was the glory that awaited on the other side.

In the pages of *He Took the Pain But Left the Memories*, I will share my plight with an illness that left me confined to a sickbed for years. There on that bed I sulked in sorrow and grief. I contemplated if God had removed his hands from my life; I wondered if I had arrived at the end of a road I knew wasn't fully traveled; and eventually, the hope that once anchored my soul became depleted until I conjured the strength to believe the words that I had spoken to so many others. In turn, that become the conduit that made hope come alive in me once more. It is that very hope I endeavor to make tangible for you in this book.

My prayer for you as you continue in this book is one with few words but deep passion: ***I pray that you find help and hope.***

# SECTION 1
# THE CALL

# CHAPTER ONE
## A DIVINE CALL TO WORSHIP

A popular worship song penned and sung by Pastor William McDowell declares, *"my life is not my own, to You I belong, I give myself - I give myself away"*. If there was a soundtrack for my life, particularly at the young age God revealed that He had plans to use me, the soundtrack would certainly include this song. I may not have known much or what being "called" actually meant beyond saying "yes" but I was sure that I belonged to the God that had desired to use me in the Earth.

Just as much as God wanted to use me, I yearned to be used by Him. I mean, who can be aware that God has perfectly formulated a role for them and wouldn't do everything in their power to fulfill that role? There can never be an honor greater or a privilege more humbling. If

8

you ask me, nothing has given my life quite the value that serving God has. In fact, it is this very call that has defined my life and my purpose. Everything I am and everything that I do is wrapped in the identity I own through Christ.

The beckoning from God was not solely about what He intended for me to do in the earth. It transcended the performing of various tasks and ministry assignments. When God decided to beckon me, he was revealing to me the form of worship He expected from me. Your role in the earth has a purpose that outweighs merely advancing the kingdom God. In essence, it is a special aroma of worship that can only come from the chosen vessel trusted with an assignment.

Our call is what solidifies our living for God and introduces us to our Maker. The second you are introduced to your maker, you have a divine collision with your purpose. Your purpose is how you will worship God in spirit and in truth.

Before God summoned me, I had not known a single one of the true doctrines of the Bible. My knowledge of God was subpar at best. I was well aware that God existed but lacked any power of revelation that would constitute a "real relationship" with him. So it's easy for you to see that the new life I had decided to give myself to was more foreign than it was familiar. In fact, it wasn't familiar at all - it just felt right; it felt like something that I was supposed to do and couldn't imagine living without doing it.

Some choose to find themselves in culture; I chose to find myself in Christ. Even at the age of 14 - an age point when most teenagers are on an exploration to discover who they really are or who they want to be - I had made Jesus my choice. I wanted nothing more than to make

Him proud. There were some individuals in the generations above me that didn't understand my motives. Some would participate in discourse that painted me as a title-chasing youth; and others felt an obligation to let me know. "It's not all that you think it is". Perhaps this was their uncanny way of protecting me and shielding me from the inevitable aspects that come with being soul out for Christ. Either way, I was sure within myself; I was sure that God was pouring out His spirit upon all people, including young people, just as He promises in Acts 2:17.

For me, it all began when my grandmother would take me to church and I would lay at the altar crying out to God for hours. My posture as a worshiper started way before I would ever grab a microphone and mount a stage to declare the word of the Lord or sing a song. Before I stood in front of a crowd, I travailed at the altar. That's important to note because sometimes many people are under the impression that having a call comes independent of being a worshipper. It does not. As a matter of truth, it goes hand in hand, it's synonymous.

Worship preserves and protects what you have been called in the earth to do. Worship is an earthly activity that engages you with a heavenly God. During worship, God exposes you to two types of truth are revealed: who you are and who He is. Further, a lifestyle of worship keeps an open line of communication with God - which is a necessity for anyone that has a relationship with God.

It was immediately evident that I was hearing things that I had NEVER heard before—and with plain scriptural proof to back up what it was that I was hearing. I remember being astonished at how clear the Bible became for me—and how much *fun* it was to study, when I had always found myself playing church with my sister and I was always the minister preaching to the family. If you are anything like the average church kid, you have had plenty of "church services" at your home , on the playground or wherever you could make it happen at...and you enjoyed every single second of it because although it was a game in a sense, it was your way of putting your love of church and for God on display. Oh, what fun!

## **KNOW** it more than you **FEEL** it

Sooner than later, I would discover that having a call and wanting to walk out my God-assigned role was deeper than makeshift church services and a "feeling". Feelings are not strong enough to be the only thing that you measure the truth that you have been called to function for God. The notion that it's solely about what you feel is misleading and not to be trusted. Let me assure each of you reading this, the definition transcends this misconstrued notion - and if you are going to be effective as a called vessel, it's extremely important that you know and understand this.

A calling from God is divine. More than a natural feeling, it is a spiritual inclination. God can speak to you directly and inform you of the purpose for which he has for you to perform. Or he can deal with you in your spirit about it. When this happens, it's likened unto fire in your bones, a passion that burns just like a violent flame in a forest fire. A burning desire to please God is directly attached to a passion that has been conceived in your spirit. For this reason, that's why even when you can't explain it, you still sense it, believe it, and maintain a strong urge to do whatever it is that God has authored on the pages of your story.

There are innumerable people of all age, backgrounds, and denominational affiliation that are puzzled over what a "calling" is. Many reduce it to little more than a particular *feeling* that comes over them, which they attribute to God. Millions in the world *feel* "called"—in some cases to the "church," in other cases to the ministry, or missionary work, and in some other cases to work with children, and yet in others to serve in the medical profession or even the military. Ignorant of what God says, so many people are left to rely on mere feelings, assuming that their lives—and the paths they choose—are divinely inspired, when that may very well be the least bit true.

The bible tells us that the formula for worship is spirit and truth. God is very particular about the manner in which worship happens. Likewise, He is just as particular in his approach to let you know what his will is for you life. It happens from a "spirit and truth" approach. If it's God leading you to function in a certain role, you can be assured that you will know it - and even if your mind carries some questions and concerns, there won't be a trace of doubt in

your spirit. Your spirit is a house for the truth so the only

proclivities that can reside there are those that are wrapped

in truth and purity.

# CHAPTER TWO
## YES- EASY TO SAY;HARD TO PAY

There is one word with 3 letters that can rearrange the course of your entire life. This word is small in word count but superlative in impact. Can you guess what that word is? If your guess is "YES", then, you are spot on. Many words have the potential to alter your life - for good or for bad - but none quite like this heavy one-liner.

Let's establish some clarity right here. A "yes" from you to God carries a major difference than one that you give to a friend, family member, spouse, or another human being. It even supersedes the one that you give to yourself. One "yes" to God changes the game...forever! The second that you say it, nothing remains the same going forward. The impact is instantaneous.

What does "YES" mean? To say yes means to agree to something; to make yourself absolutely available at all costs, to give your full commitment without recanting or backing down. When you say yes to do something, it oftentimes comes with a lot of fear attached to it, especially if what you are agreeing to is something that seems to be much bigger than you are. When God asks something of us, more often than not, what he wants us to do is outside of our comfort zone or it is something that we feel like we are not qualified to do.

The power of agreement is so real and dangerous, it will have you climbing a mountain prepared to sacrifice your one and only son. Not just a son, but the son that was given to you as a promise from God after you spent years upon years praying for him and believing that God would honor your faith. You will find yourself at that mountain ready to lay your son down at the altar as a living sacrifice, not because you want to but simply because you told God that you would. Just ask Abraham.

Next to Abraham, there's Mary. The only differentiation between the two was that Abraham had to sacrifice a son, Mary was petitioned to give birth to one. The similarities between the two? One "yes" changed everything and placed them in the middle of a foggy fear that made maneuvering hard.

At the time the angel of the Lord came to visit her with the petition to carry the son of man, she immediately became confused, unsure, overwhelmed, and questioned how someone like herself could be asked to give birth to a sovereign miracle. More than feeling inadequate to be the one chosen for this, she was overwhelmed with deep worry about how life was about to become inexplicably different.

Have you ever consider the consequences and gravity of the decision standing in front of your face, and all you were able to do is look for every question and excuse to get out of it? That was Mary. On one hand, I'm sure she felt elated to even be considered to be the carrier of a miracle of that magnitude. On the other hand, however, I am sure a "no" was what she wanted to give God. Yet, she humbly agreed. Knowing only a minuscule amount of information concerning what she was about to embark on, she made herself available at all costs. Mary didn't know the full cost, but she rendered a sure answer to the will of God nonetheless.

I guess what I'm trying to get you to understand is: you can never fully determine everything that awaits you on the flip side of your agreement. There will be unknown details, unimaginable twists and turns, lonely days, too many questions to count, days spent in between the mountains and valleys of life. Even in all of that, you have to make yourself like a tree planted by the waters. Trees are not easily moved. A tree may bend and blow with the wind but it will rarely bow under the pressure. Simply because they were created with tenacity. If God can equip a tree with roots that keep them grounded, surely there is something at your core to anchor you. You have a tenacity down inside of you that's powerful enough to sustain any commitment that you make to God.

****

Many years ago, when I gave God my word, I didn't truly understand what I was doing. Yes, I wanted to do everything that He was leading me to do but I lacked full understanding of what honoring such a commitment would entail. It all started with much excitement and enjoyment for me. It was out of the ordinary and new but I couldn't be more confident that I had made the right choice; and there was no doubt that God was with me.

Early on, I was able to get a firm grip on opportunities beyond my imagination. Week after week, I was traveling. I was going to places that were both near and far, doing the things that I was passionate about and chosen to do. It was rewarding. It was refreshing. And to be doing these things at such a young age, I knew without an inkling of doubt that God had paved this path for my feet to blaze.

Who knew that a young boy like myself would have the luxury of traveling the world? Who knew that I would be given chances to speak to diverse audiences full of young people and older people, too? I have so many memories from my beginning days. I remember accomplishing things like singing background vocals for Bishop Hezekiah Walker & The Love Fellowship Choir. I can remember having weekends completely dedicated to preaching in places where I was invited to come because someone had recognized the gift that God had given me to carry.

Let me take you through a brief walk down memory lane to give you a vivid look into what life was like for me when it all began. It was beautiful. I felt so fulfilled. On March 8th, 1992, I mounted the pulpit in front of a crowded room. The eager audience of approximately 500 people had no sitting room as everyone came to witness me speak God's word. This wasn't the norm in our culture nor church, so of course, the motivation for many to come was to see just how real it was. It was my mother's birthday; I was 14 years old, and the move of God that went forth resulted in 14 souls receiving the precious gift of salvation. If this was any indication of what was to come, I was ready to move forward in the direction God was leading me.

Now, fast forward a little bit. Another memorable moment was a power-packed revival I was honored to be a part of in North Carolina. I saw the revivals on television, I even went to a few of them, but there was nothing compared to preaching at one for the first time. Once again, God did what only His power and spirit could accomplish. By the end of the revival, an estimate of 43 souls were added to God's divine list of sons and daughters. There were many people that came to me afterwards and told me how their life had been impacted. The testimonies ranged from "I wouldn't have gotten saved if it weren't for God using you" to "you have inspired me to be better".

As you can clearly see, God's goodness was evidenced through the fruit that was coming from my ministry involvements. I was overwhelmed with a sense of accomplishment knowing that the God who reigns in Heaven wanted to use me in a great way here on earth. Over and over, God showed Himself faithful, He continued to give signs that made me realize that this way of life was the best way and that it was absolutely worth it. Wondering if God was pleased was nothing I had to spend my time doing because the proof that He was could be found easily without searching.

# SECTION 2
# THE
# CONDITION

# CHAPTER THREE
## WHEN FAVOR DOESN'T SEEM SO FAVORABLE

*Luke 12:48 NIV But the one who does not know and does things deserving punishment will be beaten with few blows. From everyone who has been given much, much will be demanded; and from the one who has been entrusted with much, much more will be asked.*

Earlier I told you that I was both a preacher and singer. My love for singing started to grown more and more. With every opportunity to tap into the musical side of me, my love for the art expanded; and eventually, I made the decision to make something of my love for singing. I made plans to record my first project. How exciting.

Everything to get the recording in motion was going according to my plans. The songs were selected, the date was set in stone, people were excited to attend, and I was so ready to see it all come into existence. The idea of having a CD added to my ministry was humbling and it reinforced the truth that God's hand was strong on my life. I felt the favor of God so mightily. I knew it was all His doing because none of it would have been an idea independent of God's favor and anointing. I felt like I could accomplish it because I knew He believed in me.

But in the midst of gearing up for what would have been another monumental point of my life, tragedy struck. Out of nowhere, everything hit an unforeseen iceberg in the middle of the water and my plans started to sink deep into the waters of despair. Instead of moving forward to record a CD, I was met with the pain of losing a loved one. My father had made his transition and I was left to deal with the disappointment of altered plans while grieving the loss of someone that added such value to my life.

I was at the hospital alone with my dad. This was right around Christmas time, a time that's designed to be full of joy, laughs, and good times. Yet, I was at the hospital unsure what the next moment would mean for me and my family. I can remember the nurses entering the room to take Pop (what I called my dad) to do a MRI procedure. As he left the room, he made a promise to me. He promised me that he would return. Minutes later, a Code Blue was issued causing him to be rushed to the ICU; and by this time, my other siblings had arrived. One hour later, he coded again, and took his final breath in front of his 5 children. I didn't get to tell him goodbye, however, right before he was taken for the MRI, I got an opportunity to do something more meaningful--invite him to accept Jesus as his personal savior and recite the Sinners Prayer with him.

Cancer was more than the cause of Pop's death; it quickly became a form of death for me as well. It felt like someone had violently ripped the heart from the chest of the little boy I was. I was broken, I was confused, and I was now fatherless.

Questions zoomed through my mind at an undetectable speed. I couldn't tell you how fast they were running through my head space but I can tell you that for every tear shed, there were an abundance of questions to match them. Why me, God? Why now? What had I, or my father, done to deserve such cruel and unusual punishment? How do I live beyond this pain? Is life even worth living still? I wrestled with understanding the position life had landed me in. This was a type of pain that I wasn't warned about; it was the kind of pain that a church cliché and scripture couldn't heal. It was real; it was strong.

I don't need to tell you that this wasn't what I had planned. It's not that a perfect life was anything I was expecting, but dealing with this level of pain was too big of a cross for my shoulders to carry at the time. My remedy to deal with it all was to do what I did best: preach my way through it. Instead of taking time off to process my father's passing, I got back on the road; I returned back to my normal routine. Instead of facing my sorrow, I decided that preaching and singing it would be the safest way for a speedy recovery. It wasn't the healing that my spirit needed but it provided a form of wholeness that made me feel complete.

Before I could properly grieve my father's passing, or should I say, before I could put a stop to trying to escape grieving my father's passing, disappointment had crept its way back into my space. About a year later, I was in Miami working with a client when I started coming down with symptoms of the flu. Thinking it was nothing major, I treated it as the flu and waited to get better. But I didn't get better. In fact, I suddenly lost my sight in one eye. It was then that I realized I needed to get to North Carolina to get the proper care.

When all of this was happening, my direct deposit hadn't come to my account so my dear friend Alicia paid my way to travel to North Carolina --totally unaware that she was helping to save my life. Upon my arrival there, I was taken to the hospital where I discovered that I had an eye infection resulting from the flu which they provided treatment for. Once again, I wasn't getting any better. Eventually, I received troubling news from my doctor that my kidneys had failed. This news didn't come years later, it came weeks later. Considering that, you might be able to determine the depth of the suffering I felt. Once again, I had questions that just seemed to lack answers sufficient enough for my plight to make sense to me.

## I WASN'T BEING TORTURED.

## I WAS A TARGET

Looking back on everything that was transpiring at that time, I can decidedly say that it all had a significant purpose for molding me. I didn't see it then but I know it now. Those experiences weren't to torture me; they weren't sent to my life by God to derail me, however, those experiences were tests given to me to see what I was made of, and to strengthen me by proving anything that my character was lacking.

The lesson learned from those two experiences is one that still resonates with me in my adult life. That is: when favor is on your life, a bull's eye is also on your back. The favor of God makes you a target by default. Favor attracts frustration. The frustration is not from God. That's so important to understand because it will spare you from believing that God has removed His grace and given you His wrath. Favor that flows from heaven touches the earth without an ounce of sorrow attached to it. Even though I was sad, sorrowful and broken, that had nothing to do with the favor on my life.

Much like Job, God allowed me endure those trials because He was confident that I would not curse Him or walk away from the call on my life. Job was faithful, upright, and deeply committed to God. There was a great presence of favor on his life. His family was prosperous, he had enormous wealth, and life was going well until he became a target to the enemy. The enemy wanted to test what Job would do if God removed the hedge that was placed around Job and his family. God, knowing that Job wouldn't curse Him to His face, removed the hedge and permitted Satan to test Job under one condition: he couldn't harm Job.

I'm not suggesting that my situation was as drastic as Job's, or even identical; but the commonality between both of our stories is that we were targets. There was a bull's eye on our back because our cups ran over with favor. I felt like I was being tortured and based on the confession that Job made, "though He slay me, yet will I trust Him", he too felt like he was enduring a dose of torture himself. But through it all, there was greater purpose that surpassed the pain of it all.

To whom much is given, much is also required. Much favor means much frustration. Much favor means that your faith will be stretched in an uncomfortable way. This is when the real cost of a yes to God is demonstrated. It is during the times of being pressed and crushed do we discover our innate potential to suffer and survive.

# CHAPTER FOUR
## A STUDENT IN SUFFERING'S CLASSROOM

While everything was happening as fast as it was, I was stunned. There were not many moments when I didn't stop to ponder "why is this happening to me, God?". I needed answers. I wanted some type of understanding that would help me feel like the pain I was enduring wasn't for naught, and that no matter how excruciating and uncomfortable it had become, it would get better eventually. There was a hope present that gave me a faith to believe that God loved me too much to let suffering be the final chapter of my story.

Suffering wasn't my end, but it was my process. At some point, God had made it very clear to me that He needed me to return to my first call in order

39

to get more glory from my life and my ministry. Our first call is the pure essence of what we have truly been sent to earth for – to suffer that glory may come to His name. Suffering has nothing to do with punishment, yet it has everything to do with allowing God to work all things together for our good.

I imagine you are reading this slightly confused, thinking to yourself, "what does being called back to suffer means?". Well, very simply, it means to be called back to, or called to, a place of heartfelt obedience. When God requires you to endure a process of suffering, He's not handing you a heap of painful events just so that you can find a way to conquer them. No, what he's really doing is, testing your limits to see how much faith you have in Him and His power; He's testing you to determine how far you are willing to go to be used for His glory, and ultimately, it's a test to prove what your true motives are by showcasing whether or not you truly have absolute love for him. As it's written in the scriptures, if you love God, you will obey His commandments by living as Jesus did (1 John 2:5-6 NIV).

How did Jesus live? The entirety of Jesus' life was spent obeying the commandments of His father. In fact, the reason that Jesus even became flesh and walked the earth was in obedience to the plan that God had for his life, so that sinners could be reconciled and given another chance to have a true relationship with God. Further, life for Jesus also meant suffering. Although he was the son of God, that fact wasn't a shield from the realities that come with human existence. Jesus experienced discomfort. Jesus experienced loss. Jesus had enemies. Jesus was crucified for the remission of sins that He wasn't responsible for. Why did He put up with all of these things? Because in addition to His love and devotion to His heavenly Father, He also loved every person that would receive grace through His suffering—that includes you; that includes me.

Everything that happened with my dad passing and my kidney's failing were written into my story with a method. There was nothing about either of those events, and every subsequent change that came with them, that was without a reason reflecting the plans that God had for my life.

## SUFFERING IS LIKE SCHOOL

A sure benefit of suffering of any kind is that it will teach you many things—this is most true when it is spiritual suffering—and that is the perspective I am addressing here. If your spirit is alert and you have an open mind to what is going on, you will be able to intake each lesson, revelation, and every bit of wisdom that undergoing suffering has to offer. In many ways, suffering is a school. There are lessons, tests, and even times for graduating. The best part of it all? There's a grace that comes with being a student in the School of Suffering. That grace gives you the ability to matriculate through each level. The only time that you'll fail is when you refuse to fight until the end. As long as you committed to fighting, you will eventually get to the finish line because with every ounce of fight you exert, God provides you with new strength that overpowers your natural strength. Strength from God becomes your shoulder to lean on when your own strength is running on empty.

I'd like to think that I was a star student in the School of Suffering, if for no other reason than the fact that I took every lesson made available. There are several lessons that stick out to me. First, the lesson of faith. When you are being tried, living with faith becomes a fight. Every second of each day is a battle to make sure that your faith makes it from one second to the next. You are literally there trying to ignore every thought that is contrary to positive, optimistic, hopeful thinking. For me, I won that battle on most days. Then, there were those days I

44

needed Jesus, my family, my peers, and even myself, to intercede and pray that my faith wouldn't fail me.

Truth be told, when you find yourself in a place of great suffering, you'll discover that faith is really all you have to cling to. What faith is and what it has the power to do becomes very real to you as you suffer. You begin to know why it is more beneficial to walk by faith and not by sight. Like the 3 Hebrews boys who were sent to the fiery furnace because they refused to bow down to a foreign God, you hold strong to your faith. Even though the flames are burning and the heat is making you uneasy, your faith says "the God I serve is able to save me." Faith sees the truth (flames) but opts to believe in a greater power (faith).

Another lesson for me, in addition to faith, involved those around me. If you are reading this and you have been living for a lengthy amount of time, you know very well that nothing reveals the characters of those around you the way that hardship does. During trying times, you will assuredly learn the heart and foundation of your most valued relationships. People, without even knowing it most times, will show you how they truly feel about you— and how they feel about what you are experiencing. To be absolutely honest, such revelations can warrant extreme heartache, especially when you have to face the hard truth that the ones you thought would be there for you are the ones that are the most distant when you need them by your side. When those you expected to push through with you become the ones to fall off, take it for what it's

46

worth—nothing more or nothing less. Their behavior is proof of one thing: *they don't fit into where God is taking you.*

***Colossians 1:23-25 NIV*** *Now I rejoice in what I am suffering for you, and I fill up in my flesh what is still lacking in regard to Christ's afflictions, for the sake of his body, which is the church. I have become its servant by the commission God gave me to present to you the word of God in its fullness*

How beautiful is it to be trusted to suffer for the sake of God's body, which is the church? What can be more of an honor than this? Just think about it for a moment—the afflictions that we meet along this journey give us temporary discomfort to bring permanent glory to God. When you ponder that fact and let it seep down into the innermost places of your being, a well of gratitude should spring forth.

All it takes is a thought!! For me, learning that had to be one of the most rewarding parts of the pain I had felt at that time of life; and even now, I still believe, with all of my heart, that there is no honor greater than being used of God in this capacity.

We, as believers, are called to take the gospel to the nations. The "nations" can mean across the globe or it can mean taking it to the person that works 2 desks away from you at your work place. You may be commissioned to travel to the local precinct or a schoolyard overseas. Either way, despite the location, no believer is exempt from the responsibility of spreading God's news across the land.

At the same time, there is no way that you can spread news about anything that you don't have any knowledge of yourself. To this end, suffering unlocks a revelation about God and His power that becomes a tool you can use to direct another soul to Christ. Because you know God intimately, and because you are no stranger to suffering, you have something to offer—something that will compel to take interest in your God, it's something that will grasp people more than a "you should try Jesus" can.

Through surviving trials and rigorous circumstances, you receive a testimony. Like the popular saying goes, "for every test there is a testimony". What is that testimony? That testimony is a personal account of the evidence of the goodness, mercy, and power of God. That testimony gives you a boldness to declare that God is real, and so is His strength and ability to save, deliver, and set the captives free.

You see, without going through anything, we won't get to truly know God. God doesn't want for us to just be saved and born again, He desires for us to have a solid relationship with him. A relationship shared with God entails days on the upside and days on the downside; it comes with afflictions and joy, but most invaluable, are the precepts and statutes that you learn. Those precepts and statutes allow you to know God, and in turn, introduce others to God.

## JUST COUNT IT JOY!

*James 1:2-3 NIV* *Consider it pure joy, my brothers and sisters, whenever you face trials of many kinds, because you know that the testing of your faith produces perseverance.*

Whatever the trials are that you end up facing, be courageous enough to count them as pure joy. There will be trials of many kinds. Heartbreak could be your trial; becoming jobless could be your trial; issues within your home could be your trial; a significant loss could be your trial. There's no limitations on the trials that may end up on your plate—but no matter what they are, still count them as pure joy. Sounds hard to do, right? I know— nevertheless, do it still.

You have one guarantee: *trouble won't last always.* The same way suffering begins it also has an end. The level of discomfort it can cause may have you thinking otherwise, but I promise you that there is an expiration date. The scriptures put it this way: the sufferings of these present times are not worth comparing to the glory that shall be revealed. What does that mean? It means that regardless of what your call to suffering brings your way, it will be momentary, not permanent, not forever, not never-ending. That's great news! That's enough encouragement to not become weary in doing good, understanding that if you do not faint, you will reap every benefit for holding on.

SECTION 3

# THE

# CONCLUSION

# CHAPTER FIVE
## I'M STILL HERE

I previously discussed my kidney failure but what I didn't tell you is just how horrible my condition was. When I arrived at the second hospital, the doctors informed me that my kidneys were functioning at an extremely low percentage of 2%. If you know anything about your kidneys and the role that they are responsible for as it pertains to being able to function and have life, you are well aware that such a low performance percentage like this meant that I was barely alive. My body was not operating on its own. Medically speaking, I was only living as a result of the life support that I had been hooked up to. Without life support and the other forms of treatment being provided, there is no

54

question as to if I would have died. As a matter of fact, the doctors had only given me a short few days to remain alive once my kidney activity declined so terribly.

Listening to the reports of the doctors, my family members had made a decision that was really unbeknownst to me considering that I was pretty much out of my mind. I was there but my ability to understand and comprehend wasn't there. My family decided that it would be best to pull the plug. Unfortunately, this seemed to be the only favorable move to make. It wasn't that they wanted me to die, but they were afraid of me spending any more time in pain. The decision to pull the plug was their way of giving a remedy for my gruesome suffering. They thought that the only way for me to be at peace was to not be laying in a hospital bed fighting to beat the sickness that had violently consumed my body.

The profession of medicine is full of trained doctors and nurses. These professionals spend years in school and programs to become proficient in their line of work. So, when they told my family to get ready to let go of me, they gave this report solely based on what they had learned and experienced during their time working with patients in my condition. At the stage of kidney failure I was on, with only 2% of kidney activity, death was sure to be my fate. Based on the way the situation looked in conjunction with what science reports give an account for, I shouldn't be writing this book for you to read right now.

## GOD CANCELLED THE FUNERAL!

When the doctors made their final decision and concluded that there was nothing left in their power to do to save me, they put me on a plane. I was being transported to Baptist Hospital in Winston Salem to die. That's right! I wasn't getting transported for a kidney transplant or another procedure that could potentially place me in a better condition; they were sending me to a new location that would have been my place of death. Upon my arrival there, I was placed on emergency dialysis while simultaneously being kept on life support. After some time, I was taken off of life support, but I didn't die although the doctors told my family that I would have to do dialysis for the rest of my life unless I was blessed enough to find a kidney donor in order to get a transplant.

Well, it's worth knowing that report was inaccurate. I'm still here. The doctors gave their report. My family was confused and there is no doubt that they loved me, but their disdain for me suffering paired with what things were looking like, they began to prepare their hearts and minds to let go of me because it honestly appeared to be the only end result….but God being the kind of God that He is, he had very different plans. The doctors gave up after they exhausted their attempts to restore my life, however, the Master Doctor was conjuring a miracle behind the scenes. God knew that what seemed like the end was not the end for me. The funeral was planned but the hand of God cancelled it.

As much as I was able to, I spent a lot of my time interacting with God while I was battling kidney failure. In the hospital, I can remember praying, singing, and just pouring the thoughts of my heart out to God. I came to the conclusion that everything was out of my control and obviously it was outside of the doctor's control, too, so the only thing for me to do was to cast my cares on a power that was greater than me and everyone else. I drew closer to God. In drawing closer, there was a sweet hope and solace that I found. Things were the furthest from okay, yet I found a confidence that let me know that things would work out for me somehow.

"This is not about you, son", were the words that God spoke to me while I was there on my sickbed. Those words came with the comforting promise that I would be healed. As a matter of fact, there was a dream I remember having while on life support. It sounds somewhat outlandish that I was actually able to dream, but I did, and I recall it rather vividly. During this dream, it was as if I was having a very personal and intimate conversation with God. I was honest and shared with Him that I wanted to be gone, I no longer wanted to stay and endure the pain and suffering that reduced me to only being able to stay alive as long as I was hooked up to a machine. So, I pleaded with God to be taken out of my misery. God listened to me but denied my request. He spoke back saying, "If I take you, they won't believe in my ability to heal."

With all of the church hurt, rejection, being walked away from, and so on, I wanted out. I didn't have a will to walk by faith. There wasn't a reason to stay, to fight, to hold on, or to believe for better....so I thought at that time. Looking back, I am so grateful that God's wisdom runs deeper than human wants. I wanted to die but God knew why I needed to live. If my prayer to be taken away from earth would have been fulfilled, I wouldn't have a personal account of God's miracle working power. It's not hard to find a person with an account of God doing something supernatural and miraculous on their behalf. You might even personally witness the hand of God at work in someone's situation around you. Yet, none of that compares to knowing for yourself. When God makes YOU the miracle that becomes all the proof that you need to believe that miracles are possible.

God's ways are better and His thoughts are higher. I'm grateful that He doesn't always comply with the desires we have because if the truth is told, a lot of what we want for ourselves is not always the best. Dying when I thought I wanted to, or when others expected me to, wouldn't of just been a quick end to my pain and suffering; that would have also prematurely ended the purpose God sent me to earth for. Everything that is convenient is not necessarily beneficial.

During the last quarter of 2014, Michelle Williams of the former girl group Destiny's Child released a song that quickly became everyone's favorite tune to ride to, workout to, or to just enjoy simply because it had a compelling beat that makes you dance even if you don't feel like it. Plus, the song has a message that reels you in as well. The message proclaims that "when Jesus says 'yes', nobody can say no." I lived those lyrics. Every bit of those lyrics were the entirety of my life. I was living proof of what a yes from GOD had the power to do. Doctors said no. Doubters said no. Medical science said no. Everything about my condition was saying no. All of those no's combined together were not strong enough to override the one yes that came from God. The song says that when Jesus says yes, nobody can say no. I want to add to that. When Jesus says yes, nobody else has to say yes. Why? Whatever God says becomes settled in Heaven and in the Earth.

## CHOOSE TO LIVE!

*Job 13:15 NIV Though he slay me, yet will I hope in him I will surely defend my ways to his face.*

*Psalms 118:17 NIV I will not die but live, and will proclaim what the LORD has done*

My plight with kidney failure made me want nothing more than to just die. All of my hope was obliterated by sickness and the exhaustion of my faith left me with a sight that didn't seem to suggest that better was possible for me.

I don't know what you may be facing right now in your personal life. Whether your battle is sickness or something else, I want to end this chapter by encouraging you to make a choice to live. Regardless of the mountain in front of you and the trials that are surrounding you, develop a desire to live. Desire to live because that is the only way you are going to see the sun break through the storm. Desire to live because if you "die" now, your tears, discomfort, and suffering would be wasted. Desire to live because you ultimately know that the goodness of the Lord is always on the other side of a downhill battle.

Living seems so hard to do when everything that should be enhancing your life is failing instead. Just like my kidneys were at 2% and failing, something in your life that is essential to your livelihood--your job, your faith, your spouse, your health, your finances, your relationships--is either inactive or functioning at such a low rate your whole quality of life is making your days colder, your pain stronger, and your peace misconstrued. Even in that, you have to choose to live. You have to choose to believe that there is more for you to gain out of life and that where you are now, though wearying and trying, is not the place where you will be subject to forever.

The same way Job made an honest choice to trust God in the face of adversity, so should you. On top of the adversity that was already doing excellent at making life a challenge, Job also had to deal with the people around him counting him out. In his ears were friends, family, and outsiders telling him to not maintain his allegiance to God; they wanted him to curse God and die...but he didn't. The whispers from the outside were trying to provoke Job into counting himself out. Instead, Job made a decision to remain still and to trust God--the God that didn't have a history of letting him down. I'm certain this choice didn't come easy and I'm sure there were moments when he wanted things to end on his terms, yet and still, his trust remained grounded.

Others might count you out, you might even count yourself out, but if God still has plans for you, those plans will manifest into reality. The next time you are laying on a bed of affliction with your faith and desire to live on life support, don't take that to mean that the end is near...don't let it be strong enough to make you not want to live on and finish the race that has been set before you. Affliction is the time to find your voice and say "I will live and not die". Affliction is the time to believe that God is up to something even though you're down to nothing.

# CHAPTER SIX
## <u>THE RECOVERY!</u>

*Job 42: 12 NIV The LORD blessed the latter part of Job's life more than the former part. He had fourteen thousand sheep, six thousand camels, a thousand yoke of oxen and a thousand donkeys.*

*1 Peter 5:10 NIV And the God of all grace, who called you to his eternal glory in Christ, after you have suffered a little while, will himself restore you and make you strong, firm and steadfast.*

As you are already aware of by reading the book, pain is ingrained within my history. My past has as many painful markings as a Dalmatian has spots. Looking back over the years, my mind can't help but to remember the variations of pain that was served on my plate. From physical illness to spiritual pain. From childhood disappointments to strained relationships with people whom I'd never expected to be at odds with. From "church hurt" to being misunderstood by people that never cared about honestly knowing me.

I have truly dealt with it all. Well, maybe not all but truly enough to know what it feels like to not be okay. I know what it's like to lose because I've lost. I know what it's like to cry because there was a time that tears were the only words I could speak. I know exactly how death bruises your core because I have loss people that were dear to my heart.

To suffer loss of any type is bitter; to experience recovery is sweet. When you are down in the pits, life is sour but when you crossover to recovery, you walk into a joy that is unspeakable; it's a joy that you can't find anywhere else and you have absolutely no reservations about where it comes from because it feels too good to flow from anywhere else but God's unending stream of provision. I know what this joy feels like. I know this joy as well as I know my first name, last name, and birthday. This joy I speak of was found in the recovery that awaited me on the other side of my trials.

Recovery is defined as a return to a normal state of health, mind, or strength. It is also defined as the action or process of regaining possession or control of something that was stolen or lost. In other words, anytime you undergo recovery, you are

70

receiving every single thing that rightfully belongs to you. That means that whatever was frustrated, stolen, or taken away will find its way back to your life. Recovery is a period of restoration. Everything is restored. Everything that was broken, damaged, or reduced, for whatever reason, becomes restored by the power of God's grace that is at work in your life. That is one of the many reasons why I love God and appreciate my past pain because through it all, when it was said and done, I was given the miracle of restoration. God thinks enough of us to always make surviving hard times worth it.

We always hear "better is the end of a thing" but I can personally attest to the power and truth behind that statement. If you are looking for proof that a greater and better life happens after going through the utmost hell-filled days, look at me, I am your proof. My life is evidence that the ending is better than the beginning. I've found it to be true that the ending matters the most. God has shown me that the latter days are blessed tremendously--so much so that, the former days won't seem to matter much at all.

I often think of Job when I think of my own experiences in life. As previously displayed throughout the book, or if you are familiar with the details of his story, you know that Job had a very trying point in his life. One day, he woke up with everything; and then there was a day that he woke up and everything was gone; and whatever remained was just as good as gone. This ordeal didn't only make life uneasy, it also made holding firm to faith impossible, and even undesirable I imagine.

Can you fathom enduring such a sudden shift in your reality? You might not even have to fathom it or spend time trying to relate to Job. For many of you reading this, you know for yourself what it's like to go downhill after becoming so comfortable on the up side of life.

When the hedge of protection was removed, Job became susceptible to Satan's tricks and schemes. However, even though the hedge was removed, there wasn't a removal of God's hand. The hand of God was still on Job, and it was upon him more powerful than it was before the hedge was lifted. We sometimes put more of faith into the "hedge" than we do the hand of God, not realizing that the hedge is merely symbolic, while the hand of God is supernatural.

The hedge that's on your life is merely similar to a gate placed around a house for the purpose of securing it. Everyone sees it and everyone knows that it belongs to you and that it's ultimately there to maintain a certain level of security. Therefore, theoretically speaking, if that gate is ever removed, people will assume that your house and yard is totally without protection, but they have no idea that on the inside of the home is an alarm system that protects the home more than the gate does.

Satan, doubters, naysayers, all thought that because the hedge had come off of Job's life that meant that anyone and anything could harm him. What they didn't know was that, although Job's material possessions and loved ones were touched, no one or nothing had authority to touch him, and if they did, it would have set off the "alarm" (God's supernatural hand).God's supernatural hand is the alarm system of our life. So, with or without a gate/hedge surrounding us, that alarm will be triggered and God will immediately come to our rescue whenever someone or something tries to do anything to us that hasn't been approved by God.

Losing my loved ones, being in the hospital fighting for my life, and having to face rigorous battles within my relationships were all forms of the hedge of my life being lifted. With every trial that came my way, the reality that the hedge was gone was impossible to ignore. You know when the hedge has been lifted because everything around you feels, looks, and seems different. However, that hedge does not leave your life unless God has demanded it to be lifted, and whenever He does that, you can be assured that there are other methods of protection and provision that are used to supplement the hedge you were once familiar with so that you are sustained and taken care of.

God is such a father in our lives. A good earthly father will make sure that their children are covered under any circumstances. A good earthly father will make provisions for whatever is lacking. The same is true for God, our loving Father in Heaven. God does the same exact thing...only in a more impactful way because He's God, and that means anything that He does is done on a larger scale that no human can compare to.

Your ending is bound to be better. The God of all grace will see to it that it is. In 1 Peter 5:10, the promise from God is: *And the God of all grace, who called you to his eternal glory in Christ, after you have suffered a little while, will himself restore you and make you strong, firm and steadfast.* Whomever endures hardship as a good soldier will reap the benefits of not throwing in the towel. Even though I couldn't see God, he saw me. He still sees me, and He is active watching over everything that involves my life. This is why I didn't give up even though I wanted to and almost did on many occasions; and this is why you can't give up now or ever.

Trust the promises of God. Never lose faith in anything that God has promised you. It will always come true. A reward of restoration is a promise that God won't forget to honor. Restoration is going to overwhelm your life the same way suffering did at one point, and when it does, everything will be better and blessed.

Your joy will be back, your peace will be back, you will get double for every bit of trouble. Believe it or not, you are going to bounce back. It is already established that you will revert back to your normal state of living and you will do so at a level higher than you have ever been on before. How amazing is it to know that we don't just come back but we come back better than ever? But you have to keep the faith and remain hopeful.

## WHY DID GOD LEAVE THE MEMORIES?

Restoration is a process that returns you to a certain level of life that once existed before trouble entered your life. It's important to know that restoration is in no way a process of elimination. Although God took away the pain and gave me back everything that I lost, the memories are still very much alive in my mind. I'm pain free but I carry the thoughts of those painful days with me today. In some moments, the memories sting, however, in most moments, the memories remind me of how good and merciful God is; they let me know that I survived what could have ended my life and some days I actually wanted to end my life.

Sometimes we shun memories because they take us back to a place mentally that we prefer not to visit again. Memories have a reason for existing, contrary to what you may think or feel at times, it's a good thing to be able to remember where you came from. When you remember your past, it motivates you to appreciate your present and expect for your future. Furthermore, remembering your past teaches you humility and gives you a cognizance about God's faithfulness when it comes to delivering and restoring.

Above anything else, my memories have a much more prevalent purpose which has created the foundation of my ministry. The memories that were left after God took the pain is the premise for the ministry I have today. My passion to restore people's hope in God and His ability to heal is directly related to the memories that are still here after God removed the pain. I am always with an urge to help someone, love someone, and be a bearer of good news to someone because I have the memories of the moments when I wanted that for myself. Because these memories run so deep, my desire to make others aware of the winner inside of them is stronger with each new day.

Scars are engraved on the skin of my chest. Every time I stare at my body, I see them. There's no avoiding it. Initially, I couldn't see it without almost becoming very depressed because it was still so fresh. With time, I've learned how to love my scars; I've learned how to see them as reminders of God's ability to redeem and restore. I see them and I see strength, I see the benefit of suffering. The scars I bear reveal that "I've learned how to suffer", and I know that *"if I suffer, I'll gain eternal life"*. Every time my eyes fall on these marks that are healed wounds, I see a tangible symbol that represents the winner that God made out of me--the same way He made a winner of Jesus after He had suffered just for the sake of humanity. And that is what makes me so glad that God took the pain, but left the memories.

# ACKNOWLEDGEMENTS

First and foremost I would like to thank God. In the process of putting this book together I realized how true this gift of writing is for me. You have given me the power to believe in my passion and pursue my dreams. I could never have done this without the faith I have in you, the Almighty.

To my mother, Irene Patterson, sister Kristen Patterson, brothers Corrie Patterson, Timothy Patterson and Brian Pate: For the first time in 36 years, I am speechless! I can barely find the words to express all the wisdom, love and support you've given me. You are my #1 fans and for that I am eternally grateful.

To my grandmother, Virginia Mclean: What can I say? I am so thankful that I have you in my corner pushing me when I am ready to give up. All the good that comes from this book I look forward to sharing with you! You are my Best friend and my Hero! Thanks for not just believing, but knowing that I could do this! I Love You Always & Forever!

To my Godparents Ronnie & Juanita, David & Debbie, Brenda Harrington and my aunts Gloria, Hazel, Deloris and Sara McLean, thank you for your support in my darkest hour. To Mesha Smith cousin aka BFF and the gifted, Dr. Earnest Pugh client/uncle away from home. Last and not least: I beg forgiveness of all those who have been with me over the course of the years and whose names I have failed to mention.

*I would like to express my gratitude to the many people who saw me through this book; to all those who provided support, talked things over, read, wrote, offered comments, allowed me to quote their remarks and assisted in the editing, proofreading and design.*

# ABOUT THE AUTHOR

Gregory Patterson is from Laurinburg, NC. It's not every day that you'll find someone who is a survivor of kidney failure and countless life battles; but Gregory Patterson is an exception.

More than a preacher, Gregory is a miracle and testament to God's healing power on a mission to restore hope and faith to anyone that cross his path.

Gregory has given his life to helping and building others. To learn more about him, his ministry, and recent events visit: http://www.gregorydpatterson.com.

Made in the USA
San Bernardino, CA
13 March 2016